RSW,00

The Essential

Guide to
SAN ROCK ART

Anne Solomon

DAVID PHILIP PUBLISHERS
Cape Town

I am grateful to the following for assistance with illustrations: Patricia and Roger de la Harpe; Shaen Adey, Dr Antonieta Jerardino; and the Manuscripts and Archives Department, Jagger Library, University of Cape Town.

First published 1998 in southern Africa by David Philip Publishers (Pty) Ltd, 208 Werdmuller Centre, Claremont 7708, South Africa

ISBN 0-86486-430-2

© 1998 Anne Solomon

Printed in South Africa by ABC Press (Pty) Ltd, 21 Kinghall Avenue, Epping, South Africa

CONTENTS

Contemporary San people, who live in the vicinity of the Kalahari Gemsbok Park. (Photo: P. de la Harpe)

INTRODUCTION

The San (sometimes known as 'Bushmen') have an African heritage of great antiquity. Their traditional lifeways – living in small bands, and travelling the landscape in search of animals to hunt and plant foods to gather – have been much modified in modern times, but are a contemporary example of the oldest known economy. San paintings and engravings on rock, one form of testimony to their long occupation of southern Africa, are amongst the most splendid in the world. San art also represents one of the longest-enduring traditions of art-making known. In the Western Cape alone, archaeologists have recorded over two and a half thousand painted sites, and many more await discovery and recording. The rock art is without doubt one of South Africa's most important cultural treasures, as well as a unique historical record.

In caves and rock shelters and across the veld are many thousands of archaeological sites belonging to the period known as the Later Stone Age. These date from approximately thirty thousand years until a few hundred years ago. Archaeologists believe that sites radiocarbon-dated to the last 10 000 years were probably made by the forerunners or ancestors of contemporary San. Stone, bone and shell artefacts and food debris, as well as skeletal remains found in such sites, have led researchers to suggest that the people who made the sites lived in much the same way as San hunter-gatherer groups in southern Africa in the twentieth century. It

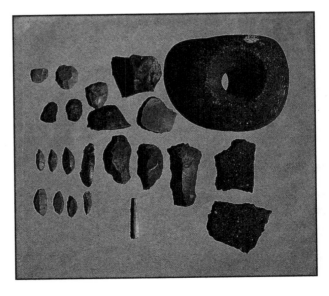

Artefacts characteristic of the Later Stone Age include bored stones (top right), scrapers, adzes and bone artefacts. Pottery (bottom right) is found in sites dating to the last 2000 years.

seems that the toolkit and way of life have been broadly continuous for as long as ten millennia. The stone artefacts are small, and designed to be attached (or hafted) to handles to make more complex tools, for cutting, scraping and other tasks. The evidence suggests that, unlike some hunter-gatherer sites which date to before 10 000 years ago, the diet of these ancestral San did not comprise very significant numbers of large animals, but that people relied on a range of smaller game, such as steenbok, tortoises, dassies, birds and the like. Coastal sites show that fish, shellfish, crayfish and marine mammals such as seals may also have been an important part of this wide-ranging diet. Along many stretches of the South African coast are great mounds of shell (which also contain stone artefacts, bone and other items), the remnants of prehistoric food-gathering.

The 'San' peoples of today are those who speak San languages. These are complex 'click' languages belonging to the Khoisan language group. (Khoi Khoe [formerly 'Hottentot'] languages also include click sounds, but have different grammatical features.) The principal San-speaking groups remaining today live in Botswana, Namibia and Angola. Their languages, although fundamentally similar, vary considerably from place to place, with scores of distinct languages and dialects known. 'San' is primarily a linguistic label, adopted by anthropologists to describe people speaking these related but distinct languages. It does not refer to physical type. The terms 'Bushman' and 'Hottentot' are now considered by many as terms of abuse. The name

'San' is often used in place of 'Bushman' (and 'Khoikhoi' or 'Khoekhoe' instead of the degrading 'Hottentot').

Many people associate 'the Bushmen' with the dwellers of the Kalahari Desert. Authors such as Laurens van der Post and Lorna Marshall, who brought the San to world attention in the 1950s, wrote about Kalahari groups with whom they lived. However, hunter-gatherers once lived all over southern Africa, and their ways of life varied accordingly. On the Cape coast, where they gathered shellfish on the beaches as part of their subsistence, they were known by the Dutch as 'Strandlopers'. Other San, living alongside rivers, relied significantly on freshwater fish. Although hunting and gathering was the basis of the lifeway, the San – experts in making the most of a variety of environments – have lived in different ways in various times and places. It was once thought that the San had been forced into the Kalahari from elsewhere as a consequence of pressure and persecution in colonial times, but archaeological evidence shows that the Kalahari San have lived in their desert environment for thousands of years.

Interest in the San once centred on the belief that they were relics of the Stone Age, 'living fossils', whose way of life would provide clues about the behaviour of early humans. This view is no longer held, although studies of hunter-gatherer peoples world-wide (in Australia and the Americas, for example) have contributed important insights about some of the ways in which human ancestors in Africa may have lived. San peoples today are as 'modern' as anyone else,

San people, no longer living the hunter-gatherer life, photographed in Salt River, Cape Town, in 1884. (Courtesy of UCT Manuscripts and Archives)

and though their economy is of great antiquity, they live in the contemporary world, not the Stone Age. The San have also been seen as original ecologists and pacifists, who treat the environment with care and respect, and whose social life is built on principles of egalitarianism and harmony. Again, these portraits of an ideal and idyllic 'original' human state are over-simplified, although it is true that the hunter-gatherer economy is ecologically gentle, and that life in small groups works against individuals acquiring power and political dominance. Although leaders are acknowledged, their power is little more than nominal, and is dependent on the support and consensus of the group.

Typically, hunter-gatherers live in bands whose members are linked by strong ties of family and kinship. Women provide the staple plant foods for their own families, as well as collecting and snaring small animals and birds. They are experts in veldcraft, skilled in the lore of medicinal plants, and providers of information about the movements of the game which they observe on their gathering expeditions. Hunting is a man's activity, and a communal effort. It is a less reliable form of food provision, and kills of large game are occasions for celebration. Rules of kinship and a strong ethic of sharing ensure that the meat is distributed to all members of the group. In general, food is not stored, because of the highly mobile lifestyle.

The band moves seasonally, especially in arid areas where availability of water may dictate that groups walk vast distances to the places where the *veldkos* grows and the herds congregate. In the lean, dry season, the group may break up into smaller family units and spread out across the landscape in the search for food. When resources are abundant, the group reunites, customarily with much celebration.

Hunting and gathering are not necessarily the onerous occupations one might imagine them to be. Even in some of the driest areas of the Kalahari, there is a seasonal abundance of resources, such as melons, berries and roots, for the skilled gatherer to collect. Research conducted in the 1960s showed that the Kalahari San spent only about half their time in the food quest, leaving ample time for the pursuit of leisure. Story-telling, music and gift-making were amongst the ways of spending spare time. Children were given a liberal and indulgent upbringing, with attention and care from many adults beyond the immediate family, few restrictions and responsibilities, and many opportunities for games and play.

The San are known as avid and animated story-tellers. The oral literature collected in the nineteenth and twentieth centuries comprises a host of humorous stories, including the comical and ridiculous doings of various well-known or notorious characters. Many stories have a more mythical or religious character, although this does not necessarily mean that they are solemn, instructional parables. The principal character in the narratives of the southern San (the San of South Africa) is a powerful being with supernatural powers, as well as a trickster who can be both malicious and absurdly stupid. Similar personalities are found in the oral traditions of the San of Botswana, Namibia and Angola. Many thousands of pages of stories were recorded in the nineteenth century from a northern Cape San group speaking a language known as /Xam (the symbol at the beginning of the word represents a particular click consonant). These /Xam stories and accounts paint a detailed and vivid picture of the ways in which the San saw their world and their existence, and have been important in providing an understanding of the imagery of the rock art.

Gift-making is another pastime, and one with important social implications. Although the band is made up of people with close family and kinship ties, these ties are also strong between different groups. Traditionally, a husband goes to live with his wife's family upon marriage, and this may involve going to live with another band. Different bands are thus usually linked through affiliations of blood. Membership of the band is flexible, and individuals or families may join up with a different group of people if they so desire. This is one mechanism whereby conflict and antagonism within a group may be defused. (Aggression is a quality much frowned upon in San societies.) Gift exchange (or *hxaro*, as it is known amongst the !Kung or Ju/'hoasi, one Kalahari group) is an important way of maintaining relationships with kin and friends elsewhere. Various items, such as strings of ostrich eggshell beads, leather goods, tortoise-shell snuff containers, and other artefacts and trinkets, are exchanged with distant kin, imposing an obligation on the recipient to reciprocate. *Hxaro* partners may exchange gifts over many years. Apart from maintaining harmonious social relationships, the network of ties may also serve as an important safety-net in times of hardship and need.

Rock painting is no longer practised by the San of today. The tradition died out in the nineteenth century in some areas, although it persisted longer in some regions than in others. Contemporary San arts – print-making, painting and other media – sometimes recall the older rock-art tradition, but also reflect the rather different world in which the San find themselves today.

Hunter-gatherer arts

Many hunter-gatherer peoples around the world were prolific makers of 'parietal' art (paintings and engravings executed in caves and shelters, and on rocks and boulders). The most famous hunter-gatherer rock art is undoubtedly that of ancient Europe, especially France, Spain and Portugal, where sites date to the Palaeolithic (the European Old Stone Age). Of these sites, the cave system of Lascaux is amongst the best known. The spectacularly beautiful and visually sophisticated art here is a source of immense pride to the French people, who take it as evidence that the great tradition of Western art may have originated in their country. Although dating all rock art is difficult (as we shall see below), scientists have managed to obtain a number of dates for European Palaeolithic art sites, which tell us that the art was made between about 12 000 and 30 000 years ago. The recent discovery of the new sites of Cosquer and Chauvet caused great excitement, and provided further evidence for the great antiquity of the origins of art-making in the distant human past.

The art of the Australian Aboriginal peoples is also renowned. Recently, it has been argued that art-making in Australia may go back as far as 50 000 years, but because of the difficulties involved in obtaining reliable dates, further research must take place before this is confirmed. Like San art, the Australian rock-painting tradition also appears to have proceeded uninterrupted for many thousands of years, and indigenous Australian artists still adorn their sacred sites today, in accordance with ancient beliefs.

Many other hunter-gatherer peoples in other parts of the world also produced large bodies of rock art. Notable examples include many American Indian groups, in both North and South America. Because America (or the New World) was populated by humans at a much later date, when a land bridge allowed people to migrate from Europe into new continents, the arts of these areas are not as ancient as those of Europe and Australia. Hunter-gatherer art is not only confined to the warmer parts of the globe. Scandinavia, for example, has many rock-art sites where images are engraved (rather than painted) onto rock faces.

There are certain similarities between the rock arts of the world. For example, red ochre was widely used as the basis for paints. A great deal of hunter-gatherer art seems to have been made as part of religious practice. Beyond these similarities, however, lie immense differences in subject, style and other features. In general, the arts of different areas need to be seen as unique and specific examples of visual expression, and of historical experience.

The antiquity of the art

How old is it? This is the question everyone asks, but only too often the answer is that we cannot tell. Dating the rock art is one of the foremost problems that researchers today wrestle with. Radiocarbon dating, as the name implies, depends on the presence of carbon for a date to be obtained. Unfortunately, the minerals used as the basis for paints are inorganic and hence contain no carbon. (Engravings, which are scraped into the rock, present even more vexing dating problems.) Although organic materials (animal and vegetable products) were probably mixed with the pigment, the amount is often too small to be analysed – either because there was too little to start with, or because it has been lost through the years. Because the environment is full of carbon, there is always a problem of contamination of the paint sample by other carbon.

In recent years, techniques have been developed which can detect tiny amounts of carbon. Figures in black paint, some of which consist mainly of charcoal, a carbon-rich substance, have been successfully dated. Where bits of organic material, such as fibres or hairs, have been included in the paint, dating has also been possible. A human figure in black paint from the south-western Cape yielded a date of approximately 500 years BP (before present), while a painting of an eland from the KwaZulu-Natal Drakensberg, which contained datable organic material, proved to be about 350 years old.

In radiocarbon dating, the pigment itself is dated directly. Unfortunately, because of the technical difficulties, direct dates remain rare, but there are other ways of establishing the age of rock art by indirect dating methods. In a site where people have lived, layers of sand or earth build up. Logically, the bottom layer is the oldest. These layers typically contain artefacts, organic materials such as bone and plant debris (if preservation is good) and charcoal from hearth and cooking fires. These organic materials can be radiocarbon dated, giving the age of the layer. On rare occasions, flakes or slabs from the wall of a painted cave become detached and fall into the layers on the site floor. Although the painted fragments themselves cannot be dated, the layer in which they are found can be, thus giving an approximate date. Of course, there is no way of knowing how long the painting was on the wall before it fell, but, logically, the painting cannot be younger than the layer in which it is found (although it may be older). This method of indirect dating can thus give a minimum age for a painting.

Although such finds are rare, two important sites have been found to contain painted slabs. At a site on the Cape west coast, large chunks of the wall of a painted cave fell into the deposits on the floor. The layer in which these painted slabs were found has been dated to approximately 3500 years ago – giving a firm indication of the minimum age of the art itself (see Chapter 4).

The oldest date for rock paintings in southern Africa comes from a Namibian cave, where painted slabs were found in deposits that could be dated. These slabs apparently did not come originally from the cave wall; along with other paintings on river pebbles and loose rocks they are known as 'portable art' or 'art mobilier'. The results were astonishing, since they indicated that the paintings were approximately 26 000–27 000 years old. No other dated rock art even approaching this age has yet been discovered in southern Africa. All the other dated art is portable art, and these finds all date to the last 10 000 years; as mentioned, sites from this time span are thought to have been created by the ancestors of the San of today.

The subjects of the paintings may also give clues to their age. Paintings and engravings of European colonists, wagons, horses, and other historical subjects cannot predate the advent of the colonial era. Horses were introduced into Natal in the nineteenth century, so paintings of them in that region must be less than two centuries old. Similarly, images of sheep and cattle, brought in by Khoi herders and black farmers respectively, cannot be older than two thousand years, when these peoples migrated into what is now South Africa.

Until we can date large numbers of paintings or engravings, we cannot tell whether the styles, subjects or forms of the art changed through time. Although it is a unique historical record, many questions remain unanswered. In the meantime, whether dated or not, the art constitutes a remarkable and spectacular part of South Africa's cultural heritage.

The rock paintings are compelling evidence of the aesthetic sensibilities and complex thought of the San. Even in the eighteenth century, travellers were astonished by the skill and beauty of the rock paintings, which challenged colonial ideas about the 'primitiveness' of the 'wild' San. Today, there is more appreciation of the cultural value of San art. Contemporary artists, in particular, have recognised this, and Walter Battiss, Pippa Skotnes, Robert Slingsby and others have celebrated it in their works.

Although the tradition of making rock art endured until the late nineteenth century in some areas, in others it did not. The turmoil of colonial times – conflict between San and colonists (and in some cases between the San and the black farmers with whom they shared the landscape) – disrupted San societies in South Africa, and destroyed their languages, traditional ways and skills. The art remains in areas they once occupied, even though the artists and their communities are long gone.

CHAPTER 1: UNDERSTANDING THE ART

Initially, San art may seem esoteric and inaccessible; the images are unfamiliar, and the visual conventions are not those of the Western art to which most of us are accustomed. Apart from gaining insights into what the images themselves represent, and why certain themes and subjects were favoured or excluded, it is important for us first to know something of the art's location and settings, the media used and the technology available.

Sites and settings

There are literally thousands of rock-art sites in South Africa alone, in all areas of the country where rock surfaces are available. Generally speaking, paintings and engravings are found in different parts of the country, and never occur in the same site. Engravings are concentrated in the north and on the interior plateau. The densest concentrations of painted sites are found in the foothills of the Drakensberg (in KwaZulu-Natal, the Eastern Cape, the Free State and Lesotho) and the south-western Cape, especially the Cederberg range and surrounding areas. Paintings are also found in the Transkei, the southern Cape, Northern Province and Mpumalanga. Although thousands of sites are known, and many have been extensively photographed and documented, others await recording, and there are unquestionably many sites still undiscovered.

Paintings are usually found in caves and shallow rock shelters, on open rock faces and large boulders. (Loose pebbles or slabs with paintings or engravings, known as 'portable art', were mentioned above; they are relatively few in number.) The areas in which engravings are found are generally less mountainous, and the art is more typically found in the open veld, on the exposed rocks with which the arid interior is strewn. Sometimes one finds a series of sites running along the banks of a river (but at other times not). Some rock-art sites – especially caves – were also living sites, which contain evidence of occupation by prehistoric peoples, but, then again, other sites are not associated with archaeological deposits or any traces of human presence whatsoever. In rock art there are very few 'rules', and the art displays extraordinary variability in almost all of its dimensions. It does seem true, though, that the artists avoided the high peaks of the mountains, preferring sites in the lower altitudes.

No two sites are ever the same. The locations of the imagery, the rock 'canvas' and the artistic choices that contribute to a site's unique character are as much a part of a painting as the painted images themselves. We know that the artists made use of various features of the rock face, and were sometimes clearly influenced by its shapes and contours when selecting the precise locations for the imagery. An unusual KwaZulu-Natal site illustrates this well. Small, rounded pebbles were trapped in the rock when it originally formed; later, natural weathering eroded the rock face, and loosened the cobbles, which fell out, leaving round impressions or holes. The San artist (or artists) painted human figures around these holes, using them to represent the stomach. In other instances, the choice of a spot may be arbitrary – or the reason for the choice may simply be beyond our capacity, in another time and culture, to understand.

Although it is not uncommon to find sites where a particularly smooth or pale patch of the rock face has been selected, while rougher, darker surrounds remain unpainted, the reverse is also true. Similarly, a seemingly suitable cave may contain no imagery whatsoever, while an apparently undistinguished rock a few metres away is covered in paintings. It seems that particular features of the landscape had specific resonances or magical significance for the artists, and purely practical or functional concerns did not necessarily govern their choices.

In a painted cave (for example), one may find figures at ankle level, or way above one's head, while paintings on the roof of a site or on the underside of a ledge are not uncommon. Sometimes the imagery is placed so high and in such an awkward spot that it seems the artists must have used a ladder of some kind. But it is important to remember that the level of a cave floor may change with time. The debris generated by daily living, together with the dust blown into a cave, may raise the floor by several metres over the years. The deposits may be washed away by water or removed by people or animals, in which case imagery which was once at eye-level appears now above one's head. Rock falls and other natural events may also change the contours of a site and create misleading impressions.

Media and technologies

Painting and engraving were the two media that San artists employed. No sites are known where an image or panel consists of both painting and engraving. The paintings tend to be better known, and have been researched more extensively than the engravings, but in both media extraordinary works of art are to be found.

Colours, pigments and paints

The colours used in the paintings are principally variants of red — including oranges, pinks and browns. These are derived from red ochre, or haematite. Yellow paints were made from yellow ochre, or limonite. Manganese oxide and plain charcoal were sources of black pigment. The nature of white pigment — the colour that preserves most poorly and is always the first to vanish — is more problematic. Gypsum and lime are two possibilities. Pigment studies and analyses are an area where developing scientific techniques have much to offer in the future. In well-preserved sites (usually a sign that they are more recent), the paint may still be present as a thick layer, but in others the paint is now no more than a stain on the surface of the rock.

A few tantalising records refer to paint-making. An account by northern Cape San (the /Xam) spoke of the places where minerals were mined as dangerous places, occupied by sorcerers. The /Xam lived in an area of the northern Cape which abounds in rock engravings, but by the 1870s no /Xam were artists any longer. One man recalled his grandfather making 'chippings', and several /Xam people provided valuable comments on paintings from elsewhere, but the practice had died out in their home terrain. In Lesotho in the 1930s, on the other hand, a Mrs How met an elderly Sotho man, Mapote, who had painted in caves alongside his San half-brothers. Mapote's account is the most detailed we have. He described the preparation of the pigments, saying that women would grind them when the moon was full. This suggests that the painting process was imbued with magical significance. Mrs How provided him with materials to demonstrate the practice of painting. Mapote specified that eland blood should be mixed with the paint, but unfortunately Mrs How could supply only ox blood. The paintings – including humans and eland – can still be seen today.

The addition of blood to the ground pigment – particularly the blood of an eland, a special creature for the San – also points to magical and symbolic ingredients being included in the paint. A liquid addition is an obvious necessity to transform pigment into a paint that can be applied. Other organic substances may also have been added to promote adhesion and binding (consistency). (Egg, vegetable extracts and urine have been suggested as possibilities.) Because they preserve poorly, and because the chemical analyses involved are extremely difficult, the nature of the binder materials used is unknown.

Little is known about 'the tools of the trade'. Paint brushes have not been found. It is possible that feathers or animal hair may have been used. Whatever it was, the artists managed to produce paintings of incredible delicacy, precision and detail. Fingers were also used for some paintings, which probably date to more recent times. We do know that in one instance, at least, paint was stored in small containers made of animal horn, since a number of these 'paint pots' were found in a cave in the Drakensberg.

Although the materials appear to be limited, even constraining, the results are testimony to the extraordinary skill and imagination of the San artists. Paintings may be monochrome (consisting of one colour only), bichrome (two colours) or polychrome (more than two). Shaded polychromes, abundant in the Drakensberg, are amongst the most visually spectacular paintings; in them, the artists used fine detail and subtle blends and gradations of colour to produce remarkable effects.

Engravings

There is a great deal less to be said about engravings, which fall into three main categories. 'Scratched' or 'scraped' engravings were made simply by scraping through the thin dark layer or patina that forms on rocks through natural weathering. 'Incised' engravings are cut more deeply into the rock, and 'pecked' engravings were made with a hammer action. The tools used are unknown, and no accounts of accompanying rituals or other practices are recorded.

As we shall see in the following chapters, there are marked differences between paintings and engravings, in subject and style. Some of these differences – but not necessarily all – may be determined by the range of technologies and processes that the various media entail.

CHAPTER 2: THE IMAGERY

Subjects

San artists in different parts of southern Africa all showed a clear preference for certain subjects: human beings and animals. Images of human figures country-wide appear in an incredible array of postures: sitting, standing, walking, running, falling, 'flying' or prostrate. Male figures appear to be more common than female figures numerically, although figures which cannot be identified as either 'male' or 'female' make up a large proportion of any total count.

The larger antelope are by far the most frequently painted animals, while (in decreasing order of frequency) birds, reptiles and insects are more rarely portrayed. The selection was undoubtedly for living things, and for the higher orders of animal. Plants – or plant-like forms – are also very rarely depicted. Almost as rare are features of the landscape or environment. The examples most commonly seen are semicircular lines which appear to represent the outline of a cave. Artefacts, such as bows, arrows and quivers, or women's digging sticks weighted with a bored stone, are sometimes associated with human figures.

Other significant categories of imagery are abstract or geometric designs, and 'historical subjects'. Geometrics and patterns, sometimes referred to as 'non-representational' figures, are far more common in the engravings. The reasons for this remain obscure. Historical subjects (those which

Rhino and elephant, from a Zimbabwean site.

Human figures, with digging sticks weighted with bored stones alongside.

belong to the period for which we have written records) comprise images which postdate colonial settlement and contact with other cultures. These include images of European settlers, wagons, horses, soldiers and, in one celebrated example from the south-western Cape, a ship, perhaps a Potuguese 'galleon'. Paintings apparently representing black farmers with knobkieries, shields or assegais, as well as depictions of cattle or sheep, can be correlated with datable historical events. Both Khoi pastoralists (who introduced fat-tailed sheep) and Iron Age Bantu-speaking farmers (who brought with them cattle and crops) migrated into South Africa about two thousand years ago.

'Non-realistic' or 'non-naturalistic' subjects – beings or things which do not exist in the mundane world – have proved important in interpretations of the art. Amongst these are figures with both human and animal characteristics – a human body and animal head, for example. Strange animals, which clearly do not represent known species, also fall into the category of 'non-naturalistic' imagery.

Many images cannot be identified at all. In some cases, poor preservation prevents us from recognising what an image might represent, and in others, where paintings are densely layered on top of one another, individual figures or panels may be impossible to distinguish. It is equally important to realise that some figures are, quite simply, unrecognisable to those who do not belong to the artists' culture or era and do not share the world-view which informs the artists' work. Since we cannot be sure how

*One of two abstract forms once described as 'Phoenician ships',
now thought by some to represent the shapes seen in hallucinatory states.*

different (historically speaking) the consciousness and culture of an artist, say five hundred years ago, may have been, it is even a matter for debate whether a San-speaker from Botswana today necessarily has better insights always into some of these images than anyone else – as one expert in contemporary San rock-art research, Professor David Lewis-Williams, has astutely observed.

Although we place images in categories or classes for the sake of convenience and practicality, art – or life – is not so easily put into boxes. Enigmatic and non-naturalistic images serve to remind students of rock art that classifications and pigeonholes reflect our own cultural, historical and individual biases. For similar reasons, numerical counts of image types are of limited use. It is important to be aware (for example) that there is only one known painting of a moth, as opposed to thousands of paintings of the largest antelope, the eland, but statistics and percentages tell us little about individual sites, panels and compositions – the real constituents of the art. After all, these are what the artists were concerned with, rather than the national average of antelope paintings, or the regional ratio of humans to animals! Classifications based on subject alone neglect colour, style, associated imagery and the placement of figures within specific sites. Combinations of imagery, styles, colours and forms are as important. Iconographic studies – those which focus narrowly on what individual images depict or represent – make a rather small contribution to our overall understanding of the art, although they are fundamental to any interpretative effort.

Style and visual devices

Across southern Africa there are some common features of style and visual effect, but variation may be more evident than consistency – especially when considering style. Style is more open to variability and imagination than the choice of subjects, which, as we shall see in Chapter 3, often seems to be determined by very specific cultural criteria. On the other hand, some stylistic and formal features, unlike the choice of subjects, are probably more constrained by technol-ogy and medium. Texture and contrast, for example, may be more important factors in engravings than paintings. Delicacy and fine lines and details are sometimes precluded by the techniques of engraving, which often works on a larger scale, and may be more important in a consideration of the paintings.

It is comparatively easy to discuss the subjects of the art in words. Style in the art is more difficult to translate, since it consists of many dimensions (colour, line, scale, composition, perspective, etc.) and is essentially visual and not verbal (hence the saying 'a picture paints a thousand words'). In the most general sense, there are some consistencies of line, space use (and, in the paintings, the widespread reliance on shades of red ochre), which, along with common subjects, create an overall impression of parallels between otherwise distinct arts. San art, in Zimbabwe, Namibia, the Drakensberg or the Cederberg, apparently draws on the same conceptual universe, even though it may vary considerably in

A human-like figure with an elaborate 'headdress'.

33

Elephants from a western Cape cave. (Photo: S. Adey)

34

A line of running figures, carrying quivers.

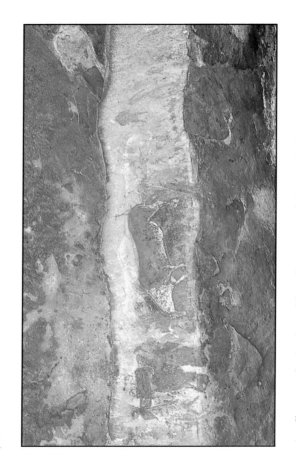

A well-preserved painted panel from Game Pass, including an eland with a human figure holding its tail.

Cattle and horses from a KwaZulu-Natal site which contains a number of images from colonial times.

Once thought of as a hunt scene, this panel is believed to portray a rain-making ritual.

Human figures in a style characteristic of Zimbabwe and Namibia.

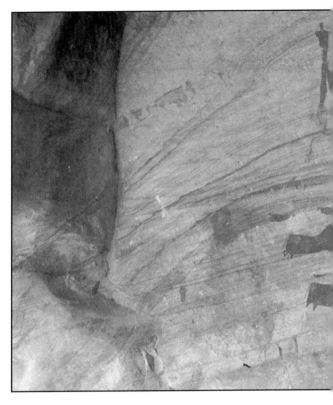

A painted panel from the Western Cape, including elongated human
leaving only the torso. (Photo: S. Adey)

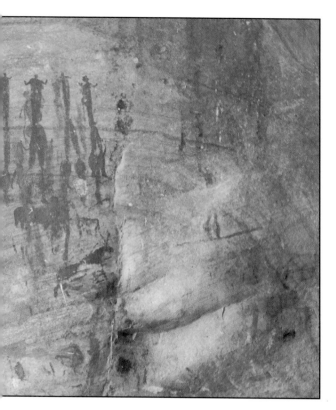

and several eland, from which the white paint has disappeared,

An engraved eland from the Northern Cape.

An eland, portrayed from the rear, using the device of foreshortening.

43

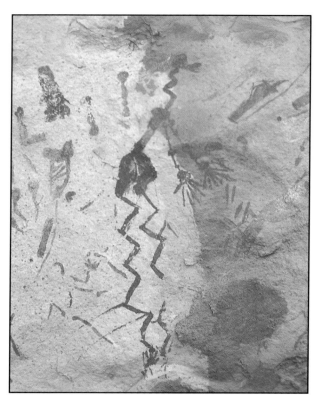

A strange figure from KwaZulu-Natal with zigzag legs and neck, as well as extra fingers.

A finely painted human figure with animal features, painted on top of other figures.

A wagon and European colonists from a Western Cape site (perhaps 18th century).

Lions and other felines may have been symbols of danger and aggression. Some may represent malevolent spirits.

A panel from KwaZulu-Natal, probably depicting female initiation, with the initiate confined in a special hut.

other ways. Styles and forms are discussed below in relation to 'variation' rather than 'common features'.

Panels and compositions

There are sites where only one or two images are to be seen. Others comprise hundreds of figures; Eland Cave in the KwaZulu-Natal Drakensberg (see Chapter 4) contains over 1600 individual figures. If one does a count, even small or 'simple' sites may turn out to consist of scores or even hundreds of figures. Although isolated figures often occur, individual images are often joined as distinct and distinctive groupings or compositions. (This is not true of all prehistoric arts.) Even to those utterly unfamiliar with the art, groups and sets of related images may be plain to see. For example, at one KwaZulu-Natal site, scores of human figures clearly belong together. They are of similar size, colour and line, and are moving in the same direction; there is no reason to doubt that they were painted at one time, or that the figures are deliberately related to one another. Formal repetition clearly links them together.

One Western Cape site contains only three separate images, in reddish-brown paint. All face towards the viewer's left. The subjects are (from left to right) a medium-sized antelope, a smaller antelope of the same general shape (presumably the young of the same species) and, behind both, a running man with a stick or club in one raised hand and a curved stick in the other. They are linked by direction, form, colour and scale, and nobody doubts that they are part of the same composition.

Other compositions achieve unity through other devices. Dancers in a panel at a site at Giant's Castle, KwaZulu-Natal, are painted in dark brown or orange. They cavort in various postures, no two the same. Yet they are organised in a roughly circular design and, although they are in different colours, clearly belong together. Even if the dance scene were rendered in black and white, the lines and visual flow would still convey the connections of one figure to another.

In practice, compositions or separate panels are not always easy to identify. In many sites, paintings are painted over others (see superimpositioning, Chapter 3), or the edges of a panel are indistinct, or panels overlap. These are but a few of the problems. However, there are some panels or groups of figures which seem to form identifiable scenes. Dance scenes are one of the principal themes found across the subcontinent. Rain-making and female initiation scenes are others. These are discussed further in the following chapter.

Variations

Theme implies variation. Regardless of common factors, the idea of 'San rock art' lumps together paintings from different times, places and environments, and from cultural traditions that may differ (a little or a lot) from one group to another. Some variations may be due to individual personalities, imagination and artistic expertise. Differences due to individual vision or preference are difficult to recognise in the archaeological record. Regional differences in the rock art are perhaps the easiest to comprehend.

I have implied that there are a number of factors – language, economy, religion and social organisation – that link otherwise diverse San groups. These – as well as technological factors and styles – account for some similarities in subjects. Nevertheless, understanding the variability in rock art – between different areas, for example – is an intriguing problem, which forces us to consider the art in all its facets.

As a subject, large buck are the most frequently painted animal in the South African art, with the eland at the top of the list. But if one looks at the art on a regional scale, this picture changes. Elephant are as popular a choice of subject in the south-western Cape as the apparently ubiquitous eland (see p. 34), yet in the Drakensberg paintings of elephants are rare. In Zimbabwe, kudu are a favoured subject, and eland are relatively uncommon. In Namibia and parts of the Northern Cape, viewers will encounter many paintings and engravings of giraffe. What do these variations in subject matter mean? As we shall see in the following chapter, the species may not be all that important: the most frequently portrayed animals are all large, herbivorous animals, which – as prey animals – have special significance in San thought. But, although art neither mirrors reality nor faithfully represents it in the tradition of documentary photography, it is not a completely separate realm. To some extent, subject choices may reflect actuality. Some regional differences in the animals portrayed undoubtedly reflect the fauna found in those areas.

In the rock art of Zimbabwe, researchers have documented images which are not found elsewhere. Strange shapes which have been dubbed 'tectoids', 'formlings' or 'ovoids' (owing to the oval shape of certain examples) continue to baffle and utterly perplex. It is possible that some may represent features of the landscape; the Zimbabwean art has more images of this kind than any other area of southern Africa, for reasons that remain obscure.

The Drakensberg paintings are renowned for their subtleties of colour, fineness of line and detail, and complexity of composition. Few sites in the south-western Cape are as elaborate. This could be the result of several factors. The Drakensberg art may comprise more recent paintings, which are therefore better preserved. On the other hand, the oldest dated art from the south-western Cape is fine and detailed work. (This suggests that we are not seeing a progressive increase in visual sophistication.) Perhaps we are looking at cultural, rather than historical, differences or preservational factors? But then consider that almost identical paintings of eland can be seen in both the Cederberg and Drakensberg, and matters become even more complicated. More secure dates will help resolve some of these perplexing questions.

One of the ways in which paintings and engravings diverge is in the high proportion of geometric or abstract designs amongst the engravings. Could it be that engraving

An enigmatic painting from Zimbabwe, one of many figures that continue to baffle researchers.

techniques, which are less suited to fine lines and detail, encouraged the artists to experiment more with patterns? What of the fact that some areas where engravings are found (Namaqualand, for example) have been long occupied by the Khoikhoi (herders and stock farmers), rather than hunter-gatherers? Could some of the dissimilarities evident in the engravings be accounted for by the fact that they were done by, or were the result of contact with, peoples practising different economic systems and with different traditions? In the same vein, might some variations relate to different classes of people? 'Crude' or roughly executed images could be evidence for a decline in the artistic tradition; or they could be the work of unskilled artists, or apprentices, or children.

Regional variability will undoubtedly become better understood when archaeologists build up more detailed local histories, and when more dates are available for the rock art itself. Understanding variability within the art is a priority of contemporary research.

Place to place: inter- and intra-site variability

Two sites only metres away from each other look entirely different. Site A is dominated by massive paintings of yellow elephants, almost a metre from trunk to tail, and well-preserved, smaller-scale paintings in the more common deep red ochre. Site B is filled with small, pinkish, faded figures – no yellow and no elephants. Why? Factors similar to those that probably underlie regional variations may explain differences between neighbouring sites: different times, contexts and preservation. Variations in subject and style are often glaring even in a single shelter – such as site A. Or are we simply seeing the work of different artists, with their own preferences, visions and skills?

Yet more complications arise. In the following chapter, we will see that historical and anthropological accounts link the production of art with ritual and ceremonial occasions, such as rain-making, initiation, curing and sorcery. It has been possible to link some kinds of scenes with some kinds of ritual events. Could differences within sites, or between those in the same small vicinity, reflect the various occasions on which art was produced?

The possibilities are legion, and the permutations and problems immensely complex, to the extent that it may seem surprising that researchers can claim any solid knowledge at all! However, some sites – or parts thereof – have proved a little easier to understand than others. Widespread and recurrent motifs and scenes – the eland and dancing figures, for example – can be correlated with accounts of belief and practice. Some interpretations which are now more or less established are discussed in detail in the next chapter. Yet many images remain obscure, and may be destined to remain mysterious.

Women dancing, in a panel from a Free State site.

Unique subjects, styles and forms

Extraordinary and unique figures are discussed less in the literature than common themes (although every image is in a sense unique, since even virtually identical figures may signify or 'work' differently, depending on their positioning and associations). A theme or motif that is frequently repeated may become more comprehensible.

For example, all signs with white borders, and a red background with the symbols S, T, O and P in white, are found at traffic intersections, and never anywhere else. It seems likely therefore that they relate to roads. If one knew of only one stop sign (and hence no pattern of associations), its function and significance would be a lot more difficult to interpret.

Similar situations often apply in the rock art. Exaggeratedly fat female figures portrayed in frontal view, although not a numerically common motif, are found all over southern Africa. Some have single or double lines (apparently streams of body fluids) associated with the genitalia. Some wield crescents, others curved or straight sticks. Some display all or most of these features. Each provides a benchmark for considering other examples.

Often, much less can be said about the multitude of images that are truly unique – except that they are unique. A moth in Eland Cave, KwaZulu-Natal, is one unique subject. Another, in a highly idiosyncratic style, is a strange human-like figure which looks rather as if it is sitting in a three-legged cooking pot. Equally bizarre is a human figure with knobbly arms, six fingers per hand, zigzag legs and neck, and a protruding tongue (p. 44). Figures like this may not be of much utility in understanding the body of San art in the wider sense and its general themes, but they are fascinating and challenging in their own right. They also perpetually remind us that while we may come ever closer to understanding the art in general terms (even sometimes in considerable detail), total understanding is an impossible dream.

CHAPTER 3: INTERPRETING THE IMAGERY

From the eighteenth century onwards, when early travellers first encountered San rock art, people have speculated on its meanings and wondered what it reveals about the lives, thoughts and histories of its makers. Ultimately, artworks cannot be reduced to words, and should be appreciated on their own terms as visual creations. On the other hand, research which explores motivations behind the art and the social and historical contexts in which it was produced (and consumed) can cast new light on images that might otherwise seem entirely inaccessible. Interpretative studies also show that art may function very differently in times and cultures beyond our own, and we need to recognise the biases that we, contemporary Westerners removed from the San world and reality, inevitably bring to our vision. A century of systematic study has brought us considerably closer to understanding many aspects of the art.

Early viewers (and some today), with little knowledge of San thought and society, interpreted the art in a purely impressionistic way. From this position have issued all sorts of speculations, some plausible and some highly eccentric. For example, a popular historical myth still lingering today is that southern Africa was once colonised by foreigners, such as Phoenicians, Hamites or, in recent pseudo-history, Indians. Today we know that these ideas are deeply flawed. Intensive archaeological, linguistic and genetic research has revealed not a trace of foreign occupation of the subcontinent by these peoples. It is also clear that the idea that foreigners were influential in southern Africa was tied to agendas which today are obviously racist. In colonial ideology both the rock art and Great Zimbabwe were considered to be far too sophisticated for 'primitive Bushmen' or black people to have created; so, the logic ran, outsiders must have been responsible. Accordingly, unusual human figures in some rock paintings were once interpreted as Phoenicians. Contemporary knowledge of southern African history and prehistory means that such imaginative speculations have no credibility, and students of rock art are not free to impose their own fantasies on the material.

Studies of the San and, especially, accounts given by San people about their world are important in this regard. From the beginnings of formal rock-art research, people have used anthropological or ethnographic knowledge to understand the art. The originator of rock-art research was George Stow, in the 1860s. He initially set out to record rock art because he feared that it was deteriorating rapidly and would soon vanish altogether. (This is true of some, but happily not much, of the art, although conservation is always a pressing concern.) Stow was in no doubt that at least some of the art was primarily of religious and spiritual significance. This insight has endured and been progressively strengthened by continuing research. Unfortunately, Stow too was occasionally prone to flights of fancy. For example, he visualised an engraving site under construction, accompanied by bizarre rituals and 'frantic orgies'.

Not surprisingly, subsequent researchers have declared themselves unimpressed with several of his ideas. Nevertheless, Stow made a powerful and permanent contribution to our understanding.

Rather than linking all the art to ritual and religion, a subsequent researcher, Dorothea Bleek, took a more prosaic view. She conceded that some of the art probably had religious significance, but suggested that it may also have served more mundane functions – perhaps 'signposts' for the hunter, or as a sign of ownership of a waterhole. Some art, people thought, was art for art's sake, or art produced for the pleasure of aesthetic creation and contemplation. While there is still value in Bleek's insistence that not all the art could be presumed to serve the same purpose, the idea that art is made purely for its own sake, or for sensory pleasure, has also been strongly contested and partly discredited. The notions that at least some of the art literally represented 'scenes from everyday life', and that paintings of animals had to with hunting (either as a factual record or as a strategy for magically influencing the outcome), are also now thought to be incorrect. By the middle of the twentieth century, the 'meaning of the art' must have seemed very elusive. At this time, interpretation did not flourish. Nevertheless, enthusiasts such as Alec Willcox, Bert Woodhouse and Neil Lee did much to promote awareness of rock art in popular books, and in recording, using the new technology of colour photography, while Townley Johnson devoted much time to producing facsimile paintings of important rock-art sites, some of which were published.

The 1970s ushered in a new phase of research and understanding. Scholars had become impatient with over-imaginative speculations and sought to be more rigorous and scientific. New attention was directed at detailed recording and statistical analysis of the numbers and types of images; Harald Pager's meticulous recording and repro-ductions of paintings remain unsurpassed today. At the same time, two researchers – Patricia Vinnicombe and David Lewis-Williams – conducted ground-breaking research using anthropological knowledge of the San and their universe. Their works are keystones of current under-standing.

Myth and rock art

In 1976 Patricia Vinnicombe published the findings from her many years of study of Drakensberg paintings in a book entitled *People of the Eland*. She explored links between the art and religious thought, especially mythology, by paying close attention to stories told by San speakers and recorded since the nineteenth century. By examining motifs in the art and comparing them with characters in the myths and nar-ratives, Vinnicombe showed that animals such as the eland unquestionably had powerful mythical and symbolic signif-icance.

The eland was the animal most dear to /Kaggen, or Cagn, the creator figure in southern San mythology. One nineteenth-century telling of the eland creation story, by a Lesotho San man named Qing, described how Cagn lovingly reared a young eland, but his sons unwittingly killed it while out hunting. An angry and distraught Cagn gathered its remains into a pot, which his wife stirred and churned. Drops of blood and fat spattered onto the ground and turned into eland; that was when meat was given to the San to hunt and eat, and that was the origin of the vast herds of eland which used to roam the land.

The place of the eland in myth and cosmology (we know from excavated food remains that it wasn't a staple on the menu) helps to explain why it is by far the most frequently portrayed creature in the art. It is unlikely that images of eland were produced either as part of hunting and the food quest, or simply as aesthetically pleasing reproductions celebrating the eland's plump beauty, which the San so admired. Rather, they are evocative symbols of religious feeling, of the creator's benevolence, and of prosperity in an ideal world.

In the same way, other animals in the art are not necessarily mere reproductions, but symbols which evoked powerful and emotive associations for the artists and their communities. Baboons, for example, were thought to be clever but malicious, while lions were symbols of aggression, and so on. The myths and stories point towards the complex of meanings attached to particular motifs, and their spiritual and social importance.

Art and myth are clearly linked. Two San men in the

nineteenth century, from Lesotho and the northern Cape respectively, commented on a set of Lesotho paintings (or copies of them). Both said that figures which combined human and animal features belonged to an earlier or ancient 'race' of San people, also called the 'First Bushmen'. These were mythical San ancestors, who lived before Creation had been completed, at a time when people and animals were undistinguished, and animals could speak like humans. Only later were they separated and ranked for ever as hunter and prey. Some of the figures known as therianthropes – figures with both human and animal features – are well explained as mythical forebears from the days when the world was being created.

Despite clear links between art and myth, the images are certainly not illustrations of scenes from the stories. There are subjects in the art which do not appear in the narratives, and vice versa. People have searched in vain for depictions of /Kaggen or Cagn, the southern San creator and trickster god. Perhaps he is portrayed, but we cannot recognise him (one of his abilities was to assume other guises, including animal form). Another possibility is that religious taboo prohibited the artists from depicting him. The stories by no means reveal all about the art. To understand more, studies focusing on ritual, rather than myth, are important.

Art and ritual

Some panels and sites have been firmly linked to important ritual events – rain-making, initiation and curing. The /Xam described their beliefs about the rain in some detail. It involved catching a 'rain animal' in its home, the waterhole. Rain-makers sought a female rain animal; the male rain animal was believed to be an extremely dangerous being. After capture, it had to be led to a high place and sacrificed, and where the blood ran, rain was said to then fall. Several painted panels are clearly to do with rain-making. Perhaps the clearest is found at Giant's Castle, KwaZulu-Natal (p. 38). It shows a large, hoofed, ox-like animal surrounded by cavorting men. There is no evidence that this is an ordinary hunt for food, and the figures are in fact dancing, not pursuing prey. Other features of the scene relate it to the supernatural. For example, a line of dots issues from the animal's neck, the place where, for humans too, supernatural potency is said to enter and exit. A strange winged creature, part bird, part animal, part human, is also known to relate to the world of the supernatural, sorcery and the spirit realm (p. 69).

Elsewhere, in paintings and engravings that are linked to rain-making, different animals, including eland, elephant, hippos and other large herbivores, take the place of the ox-like rain animal. Some of these mythical creatures are fantasy animals, bearing no resemblance to living animals. Kalahari San in the 1950s and 1960s explained that the large, herbivorous animals, like humans, possess a supernatural potency called *!now*, linked to birth and death, and good or bad weather. These beliefs go some way to explaining why other animals were less favoured subjects for the artists.

Another ritual, of which the /Xam a century ago spoke extensively, is female initiation. Accounts of this ceremony among San groups in the Kalahari in the 1950s and later tell us even more about this important event. A young woman initiated at puberty would be confined in a special initiate's hut for some days, covered in a skin kaross, and obliged to observe food restrictions. She was not allowed to go near the water, or the male rain might catch her, then drown her and her family. Special songs were sung and dances performed. The initiate's release was a joyous occasion, after which she assumed the duties of adult life. A Drakensberg painting which corresponds closely to these accounts shows a hut, containing a figure apparently covered with a kaross, and two clapping figures (p. 48). Circling the hut are more clapping and dancing figures. The girl's dance in the Kalahari was called the Great Eland Dance; and in the centre of the panel, below the hut and dancers, there is an eland. A recurrent motif of exaggeratedly fat female figures with crescent-shaped sticks and 'streams' or emissions from the genitalia probably also relates to initiation.

A great deal has been written in recent years about the connections between healing or medicine rituals and the making of the rock art. Lewis-Williams and his colleagues argue that the curing ritual is the most important of all. In the Kalahari, healing takes place at special dances. The rhythm of the dance and the medicine songs sung by clapping women send the medicine people into a trance state. In deep trance, people may collapse unconscious. In trance, healers believe that they travel to the spirit world where they do battle with the spirits who shoot 'arrows of sickness' into people.

Lewis-Williams's interpretation stresses the hallucinations experienced in the trance state; he and others believe that the visions which the healer (or 'shaman') sees are the inspiration for the art and its forms. Geometric forms and abstract designs known to occur in the art – especially the engravings – are said to represent shapes and patterns universally characteristic of visual hallucinations. All manner of other images have been explained as hallucinatory, including distorted and bizarre human figures, strange animals and much more. Many of the dance scenes are convincingly explained as straightforward portrayals of healing dances, where seated women clap and sing powerful medicine songs, and medicine people dance in a circle around the night fire.

A number of researchers believe that all the artists were shamans who painted and engraved their visions on to rock as a way of communicating their religious experiences, and that almost all of the art is of shamanic origin. But knowledge of the spirit world would have been known to all from childhood. Trance is not a requirement for producing visual art, and it is entirely possible that any adult familiar with the mythology about the spirit world and beliefs about the healing ritual, and who possessed artistic skill and imagination, may have been an artist.

Therianthropes (figures both human and animal) are said by some researchers to depict the trancing shaman's experience of turning into an animal. On the other hand, the two San men interviewed in the nineteenth century both linked these figures to the mythical 'people of the early race', or 'First Bushmen'. Some therianthropes may depict the spirits of the dead mentioned frequently by the /Xam. Some dances – those consisting only of women, for example – are perhaps more plausibly linked to initiation. Finally, it seems very unlikely that the forms allegedly generated by the nervous system in altered states can account for the enormous diversity in the art – in subjects, styles and forms. Trance may be an important influence, or thread, but does not explain the imagery of all times and places.

Regardless of the extent to which one accepts the importance of hallucinations in explaining the art, the 'shamanistic model' has provided further firm evidence for the importance of religious thought in understanding the art. Yet the San see no clear dividing line between religious and secular life. There is magic and sorcery in the everyday, and throughout the landscape. Rather than seeing everything as originating in trance, we may see the rock art as a body of work which arises in everyday life, and which deals with its problems and pleasures in a variety of ways.

Strange figures, which are thought to relate to religious belief and ritual practice.

Everyday life, society and history

Before the symbolism of the imagery was well established, some authors interpreted the art in a very literal way, as a record of activities; and indeed, some images do seem to portray real events – paintings of dances, for instance. Accordingly, scenes of men and animals were interpreted as illustrations of the hunt for food. But, as Lewis-Williams has pointed out, very few such scenes are convincing portrayals of hunts. In many alleged 'hunting scenes', the prey seems to be a rain animal, not the next meal. Controversy has also raged over humans with animal features, with some writers making a case for them as representing 'real' people disguised with animal masks for hunting, or in animal costumes donned for ritual occasions, whereas the shamanists believe that they represent trancers' hallucinatory sensations of themselves fused with various potent animals.

In a body of art as diverse as the San's, we should be careful about generalisations. Two apparently similar images do not necessarily represent the self-same thing. Therianthropic figures may represent mythical ancestors, spirits of the dead, disguised hunters, people in ritual costume or trance experience. Each example should be considered individually on its own merits. Although many panels have a very strong religious flavour, not all necessarily derive directly from myth and ritual. What can the art tell us about life as it was lived day to day, and about the 'real' experiences of San communities?

One of the features of San art is that men and women are often depicted in separate panels, or as separate groups in the same panel. This clearly mirrors the division of the sexes in San societies, where male and female roles, like hunting and gathering, are clearly defined. At group dances, for example, men and women participate in same-sex groups, not as couples. Beliefs about gender are not only basic to what people do and how they behave on a daily basis, but strongly structure other beliefs, such as those about the rain. However, the art is not a direct source of social information. Children are rare subjects, although they are depicted, for example, being carried on the back.

The images which can be linked to known events may provide historical information. One of the best known is the so-called galleon from the south-western Cape. It depicts a ship with four masts; each has a flag flying from the top. In defiance of the laws of physics, three of the flags blow in one direction and the fourth in another! Although the painting is not so detailed that its type can be easily identified, it has been suggested that it is of a kind that was used by Portuguese navigators. Other paintings and engravings also record San observations of the encroaching colonial order. A renowned Western Cape site contains panels which show wagons, horses or donkeys, men with guns and women in long, patterned dresses. Engravings in the north quite commonly include images of farmers with hats and other European artefacts, and wagons are also recorded in Drakensberg paintings.

Soldiers are an occasional motif in the KwaZulu-Natal art, with one so accurately painted that his regiment can be tentatively identified. Another painting shows a soldier firing into a tumultuous group of San, some of whom are on horseback; his target sprawls, the bullet having apparently found its mark. Paintings of San and horses can be linked to the conflict-filled nineteenth century, when the San became expert horse and stock thieves, as well as skilled riders. Raids and counter-raids by colonists are well documented in writings of the time. Images of fat-tailed sheep and cattle, introduced by the Khoi and Iron Age farmers respectively, and paintings of warriors with assegais and shields, also provide historical information, and testify to trade and interaction between San groups and their various neighbours.

Although paintings of historical subjects can be correlated with historical events, this does not necessarily mean that they do not have a magical component. It has been suggested that some such scenes also relate to trance and to magical means of resolving the problems encountered in colonial times. We cannot say for certain that images of this kind were a literal record of actual events, although they clearly show the San's familiarity with trekkers, soldiers, guns and so on. Also, until the problem of dating the art is further resolved, the direct historical information which the art provides will remain limited.

Form and understanding the art

Art historians emphasise the point that visual devices (style, form, composition, colour, placement, etc.) also convey 'meaning'; and that studies which describe and identify the imagery do not assign enough importance to rock art as a visual medium, first and foremost. Studies of this kind have become more important in recent years. One such way in which people have tried to interpret the art is by studies of superimpositioning – examining the ways in which paintings are layered over other paintings. Results suggest that this was probably a deliberate strategy, since only certain types of images are painted over or under certain other types of images. Colour use probably also conveyed meaning. For example, some figures, which may represent spirits, are executed in white – perhaps the colour of death, as in other African societies. Red paint may have functioned as symbolic blood. Some researchers have tried to link certain kinds of compositions with the trance experience and sensations of disorientation. Although accessing 'meanings' through formal studies is in its infancy, these approaches promise to extend our understanding in the future.

CHAPTER 4: SOME SPECIAL SITES

Certain sites have been of particular importance in rock-art research, for a variety of reasons – their archaeological or historical significance, their importance in understanding the meaning of the art, or their visual splendour. A few of the paintings from some of these sites, and the sites themselves, are discussed briefly here.

The oldest dated paintings in South Africa: a west coast cave

A site on the Cape west coast, excavated by Dr Antonieta Jerardino and Royden Yates, has yielded one of the most exciting finds in recent rock-art research: a series of painted slabs that have fallen off the wall into the deposits on the cave floor. The excavation showed that there had been a fire in the cave in the past, and it is thought that the heat caused large chunks of the wall to 'pop' off. The levels in which the painted slabs were found are dated to about 3500 years ago. The painted slabs from the west coast are important in several ways. Not only are they the oldest wall paintings (as opposed to 'portable' art) yet found in South Africa, but their delicate rendering has important implications.

The paintings depict a line of human figures, probably male. They are painted in red ochre, with white details – namely, very fine white lines and dots on the figure's knees and ankles. The importance of this find relates to questions

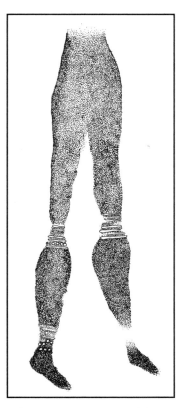

Schematic representation of the remnants of a human figure with decorated knees and ankles, dated to 3500 years ago.

about style and antiquity. It used to be thought that the paintings may have developed or 'evolved' from simple, monochrome figures to more complex multi-coloured figures, using fine lines. The finds from this cave show that such delicate brushwork is not necessarily a more recent development. The painted slabs are crucial for our understanding of style and the history of rock painting. Similar paintings are still to be seen on cave walls in the south-western Cape, and, although no scientific proof is available as yet, it suggests that some of the finely executed paintings still visible today may be of similar antiquity.

A visual feast: Eland Cave

In KwaZulu-Natal there is one of the most densely painted sites known. Eland Cave, in the Cathedral Peak area, contains over 1600 painted images, and an extraordinary range of styles and subjects. It is also one of the most spectacular sites in terms of its conformation and location. It is a large and relatively deep cave, which offers substantial shelter. It also seems to have been a living site, with deposits containing the debris of everyday life still present on the cave floor. A waterfall flows over the roof and down into the deep valley below. The imagery contains many rare, even unique images, including an aardwolf (*Proteles cristatus*) and a moth – one of the few examples of insects in the rock art. Many of the paintings are beautifully preserved, although the scars left by vandals, who tried unsuccessfully to quarry panels out in the earlier years of the twentieth century, are starkly apparent.

A spectacular frieze of shaded polychrome eland gave the site its name, but there are many other equally notable paintings to be seen. These include a finely painted lion (p. 47), associated with other animals, and a strange human figure with an elaborate headdress (p. 33). Lions are thought to be symbols of danger and aggression. Some may represent powerful and dangerous people or spirits, as may some other strange, non-realistic human figures. The excellent preservation of these and other paintings at Eland Cave suggests that at least some of the paintings here are relatively recent (at an educated guess, dating to not more than half a century or so ago). The visual splendour of this site makes it one of the most important of the thousands of sites known. Like all rock art sites, it is protected by law (the National Monuments Act). Its location in one of the Natal Parks Board reserves offers hope for its protection – unlike many other sites, which fall prey to both unthinking and deliberate vandalism.

Game Pass: magic and the supernatural

Rock art presents great difficulties of management. Game Pass, with its vivid and complex paintings, has been fenced off, and access is only permitted to those accompanied by a Natal Parks Board guide. The site contains some of the most elaborate and beautiful paintings known in South Africa.

One of the most celebrated panels shows an eland, with the hair on its neck standing on end, and its legs crossed. Its lowered head and other features suggest that it is dying. A human figure holds its tail; he too has his legs crossed (p. 36), apparently in imitation. It has been argued that this figure is a shaman, medicine man or sorcerer. Other paintings in the site depict large human figures wearing cloaks or karosses; these figures are also painted in close association with remarkably fine, shaded polychrome eland. Dr Patricia Vinnicombe, one of the pioneer researchers of Drakensberg rock art, thought that such figures represented medicine people, a view reiterated by Professor David Lewis-Williams of the University of the Witwatersrand.

Although this site has been at least partly protected from human interference and damage, and is extraordinarily well preserved, paintings such as this remain at risk from the elements, from the sun and from the natural decay of the rock. The processes of natural decay are very variable and extremely complex. They remaily poorly understood, although geochemists continue to study the factors involved.

The impact of colonialism: historical imagery in KwaZulu-Natal

It is thought that the tradition of rock painting endured longer in parts of the KwaZulu-Natal Drakensberg than in other parts of the country. Sites in this region contain many images which clearly relate to colonial times. One site in the southern Drakensberg is particularly rich in imagery from this time period (p. 37). It is a long, shallow rock shelter, rather than a cave where people lived, and contains paintings in a variety of styles and colours. The paintings include horses, cattle and mounted San, and must date to the nineteenth century. Other panels in the site, including dances and human figures, do not include images that give clues to their antiquity, and these may or may not be older. Many of the images which date to the nineteenth century are well preserved; other scenes, painted in black, are extremely faded and, in some cases, barely visible. It seems that, like others, this site may have been visited repeatedly, perhaps over hundreds of years, with different artists adding to the existing imagery at different times. Unfortunately, this includes contemporary graffiti – including some, dating to the 1980s, in Chinese characters!

CONCLUSION

Both paintings and engravings are on display in museums in the various centres, but the rock art is best appreciated in its original setting. Although some of the art is in remote and inaccessible areas, there are a number of places where it can be visited without a lengthy trek. By a happy coincidence, some of the most visually impressive paintings occur in nature and game reserves (for example, those managed by the Natal Parks Board). Branches of the South African Archaeological Society country-wide organise field trips to view the art as well as a wide range of other archaeological sites.

Even faded or otherwise unspectacular sites are important for research into the rock art. There are certain precautions to take to prevent its deterioration. It should never be wetted, or touched with the fingers; fires should not be lit where smoke can reach it; and, of course, adding one's own contribution is illegal.

Many amateurs and outdoor enthusiasts have contributed substantially to our knowledge of the art by finding and recording previously unknown sites. Colour photography is the best recording method, although the art can be surprisingly difficult to photograph; it may require balancing precariously on narrow ledges, or lying face-down in the dirt. Flash photography does not damage the paintings, although use of a flash 'flattens' the rock face and reduces its textural qualities. Available light is often adequate.